Perhaps the most important single element in building and maintaining guitar technique is the daily and systematic study of scales. This text is the approach I have used and taught for years. Scales are broken into segments (major and minor) and are thoroughly applied on all strings in all positions. Chromatic and whole tone studies are included. Finally, this approach to scales integrates scale relationships through many exercises and studies.

It is essential for the guitarist to strive for smoothness and continuity in playing scales. Avoid choppiness and ragged performance. Do not play the scales faster than you can clearly perform them. Technique is developed by playing scales smoothly at slow speed before accelerating to faster tempos. Keep both left and right hands relaxed at all times and avoid jerky or sudden movements in changing positions. Finally, in order to successfully practice scales, you must play them from memory. Diligence and patience in studying scales are the gateways to polished, flowing performance on the guitar.

1 2 3 4 5 6 7 8 9 0

Mel Bay

The Major Scales on the 6th, 5th and 4th Strings
(One Octave)

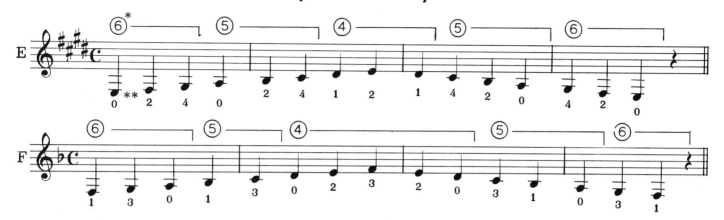

The following pattern will be used to play major scales up the fingerboard.

This should be memorized and played up the fingerboard as high as feasible.

Roman numerals indicate the positions.

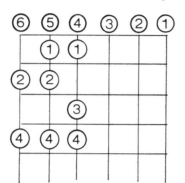

Play the following in

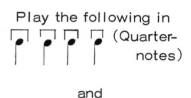 (Quarter-notes)

and

 (Eighth-notes)

The classic guitarist should use the R.H. patterns indicated on page **4**.

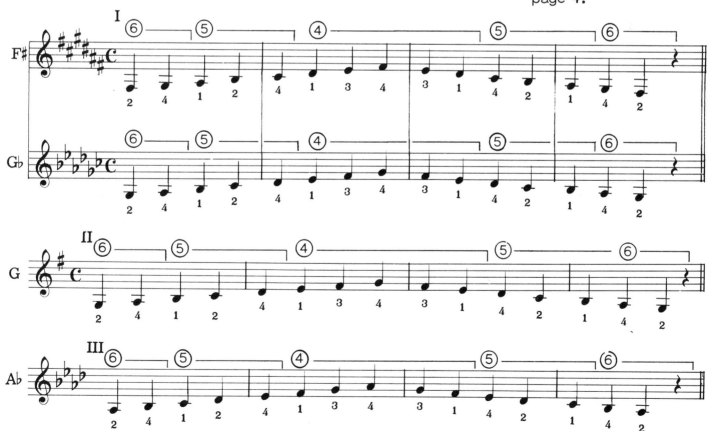

*Numbers in circles indicate string.   **Numbers below notes indicate fingering.

4

**CLASSIC GUITAR RIGHT HAND FINGERING
PATTERNS SHOULD BE AS FOLLOWS:**

p-i, i-p, i-m, m-i, m-a, a-m, p-i-m-a, a-m-i-p.

Minor Scale Modes
NATURAL (PURE)

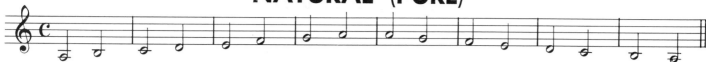

HARMONIC

The 7th tone is raised one half-step ascending and descending.

The above mode will be the minor scale used in this book. The performer may use the other modes by adhering to the structure as indicated.

MELODIC

The 6th and 7th tones are raised one half-step ascending and lowered back to their normal pitch descending.

THE GYPSY MINOR SCALE

This colorful and widely used scale is created by raising the fourth and seventh degrees ½ step.

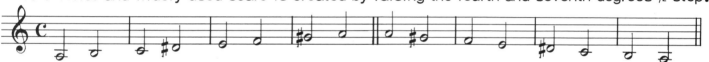

Each Major key will have a <u>Relative Minor</u> key.

The <u>Relative Minor</u> Scale is built upon the *sixth tone* of the Major Scale.

The Key Signature of both will be the same.

The Minor Scale will have the same number of tones (7) as the Major.

The difference between the two scales is the arrangement of the whole-steps and half-steps.

THE TONIC MINOR SCALE

Lowering the third and sixth degrees of a major scale will create a Harmonic Minor scale. This is done extensively by composers. This is referred to as the Tonic Minor scale since both scales are built on the Tonic Tone (1).

TONIC MINOR

6

The Minor Scales on the 6th, 5th and 4th Strings
(Harmonic Mode)

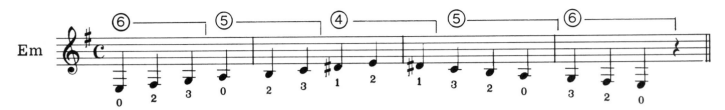

The following pattern will be employed in playing the minor scales up the fingerboard. (Harmonic mode - one octave)

Memorize and play up the fingerboard as high as possible.

Roman numerals indicate the positions.

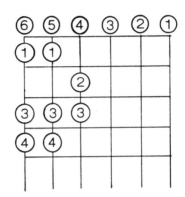

Play first in quarter notes. When memorized play as eighth notes.

Use same plectrum strokes as indicated for the major scales.

Classic players employ same R.H. finger patterns as in the major scales.

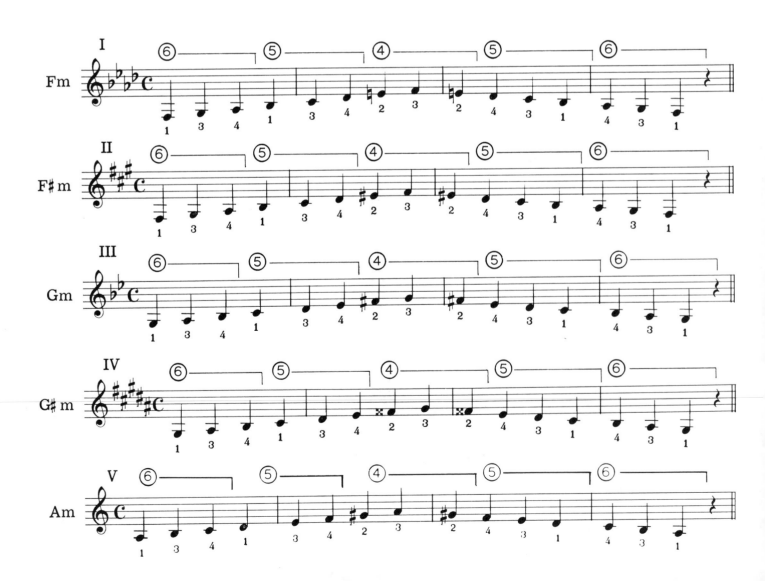

TETRACHORDS

A TETRACHORD is a four tone scale arranged in the following sequence:

Whole-step, whole-step, half-step. (1, 1, ½)

Each major scale is made up of two tetrachords as shown in the example:

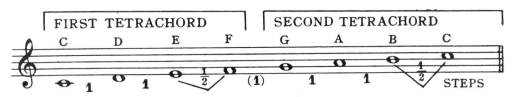

The two tetrachords in the major scales are separated by one whole-step.

The Major to Tonic Minor Scales on the 6th, 5th and 4th Strings

(Harmonic Mode)

Continue the above as high as the guitar will permit

The Major to Relative Minor Scales on the 6th, 5th and 4th Strings

(Harmonic Mode)

The Major Scales on the 5th, 4th and 3rd Strings

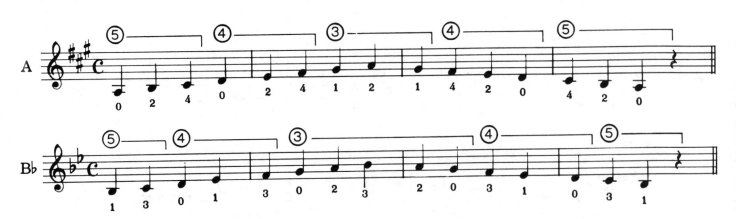

Play the following pattern up the fingerboard to produce the scales as indicated

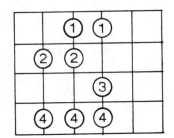

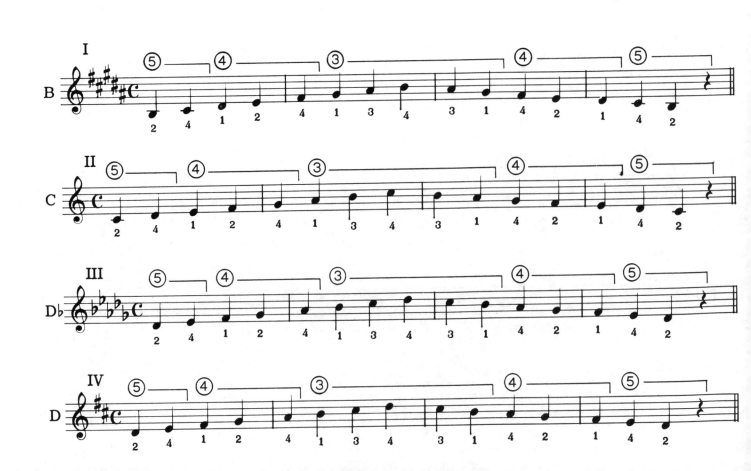

RELATED KEYS

The first tetrachord of the C scale will be the same as the last tetrachord of the F scale. The second tetrachord of the C scale is the same as the first tetrachord of the G scale.

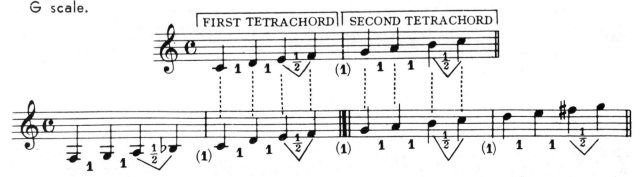

The Harmonic Mode Minor Scales on the 5th, 4th and 3rd Strings

Am

Play the following pattern up the fingerboard to produce the scales as indicated

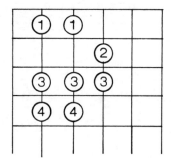

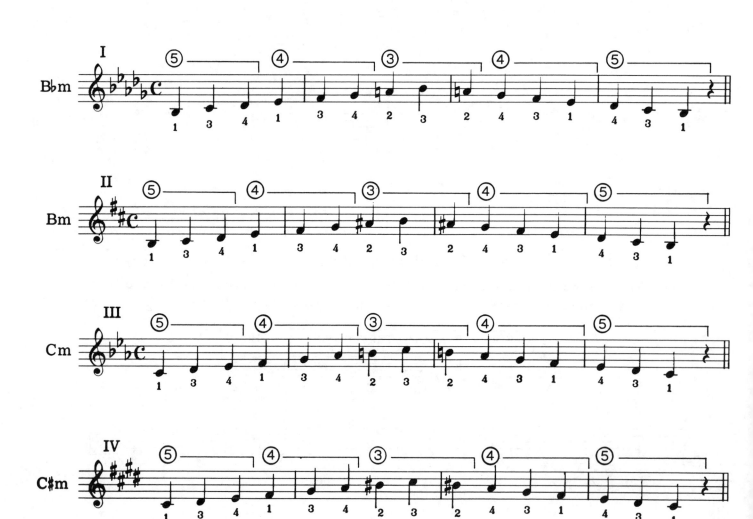

The Major to Tonic Minor Scales on the 5th, 4th, 3rd and 2nd Strings
(Harmonic Mode)

Continue upward if the range of the instrument permits

The Major to Relative Minor Scales on the 5th, 4th and 3rd Strings

The Major Scales on the 6th, 5th, 4th and 3rd Strings

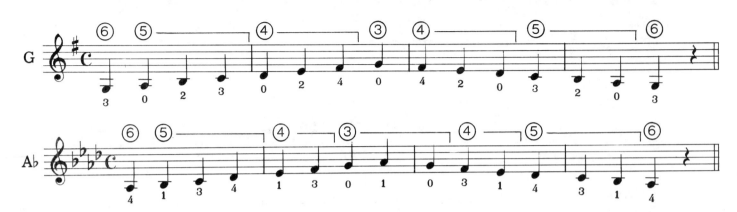

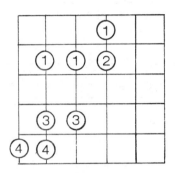

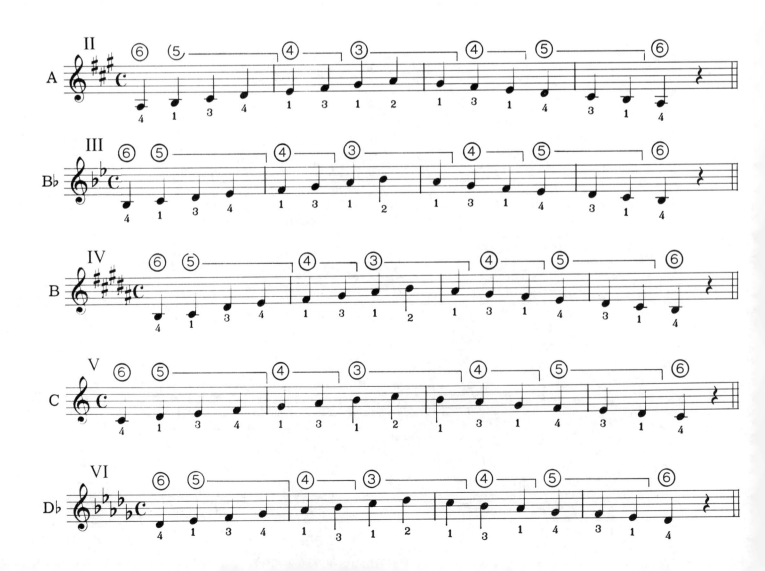

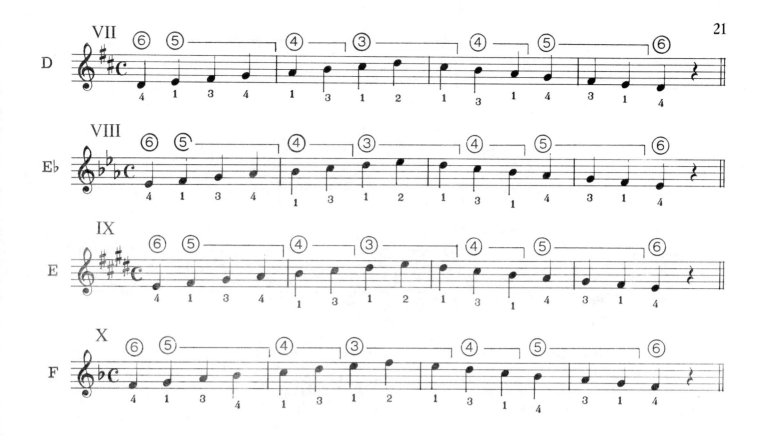

The Minor Scales on the 6th, 5th, 4th and 3rd Strings

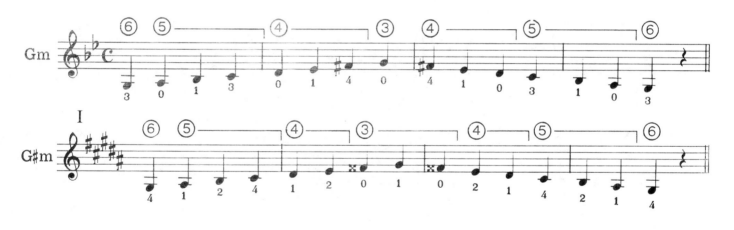

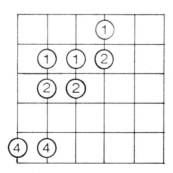

22

The Major to Tonic Minor Scales on the 6th, 5th, 4th and 3rd Strings

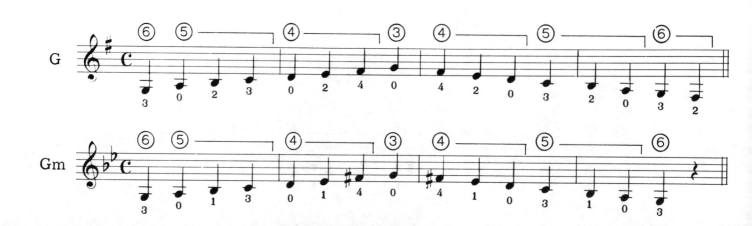

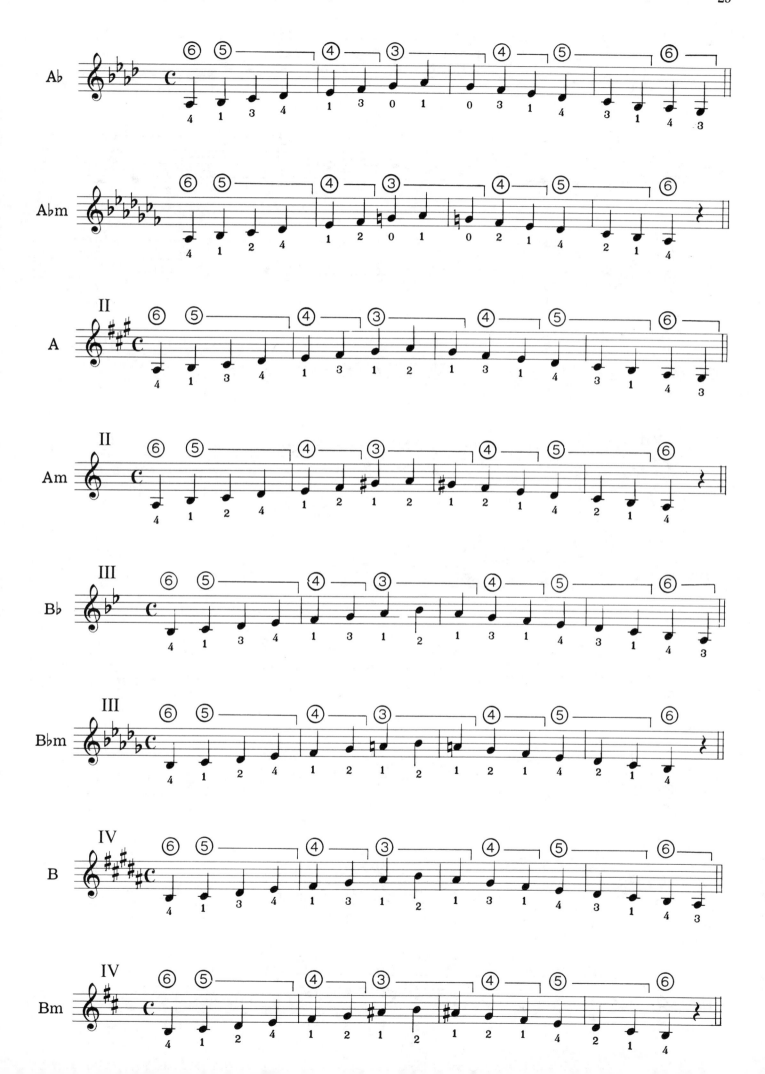

The Major to Relative Minor Scales on the 6th, 5th, 4th and 3rd Strings

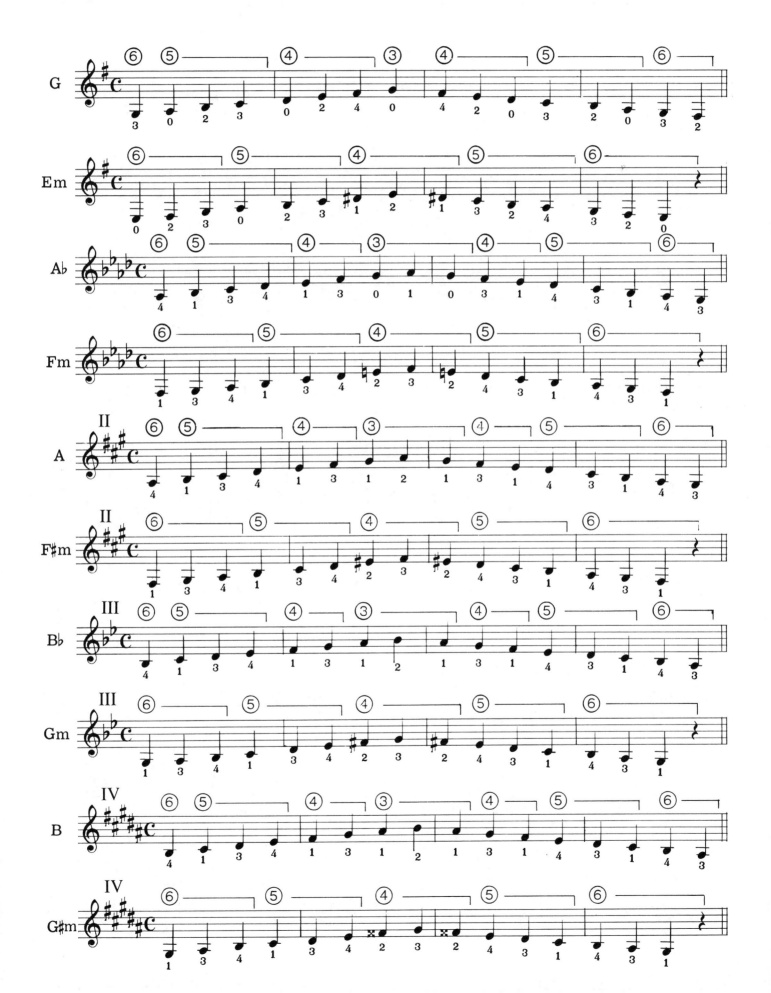

The Major Scales on the 5th, 4th, 3rd and 2nd Strings

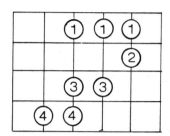

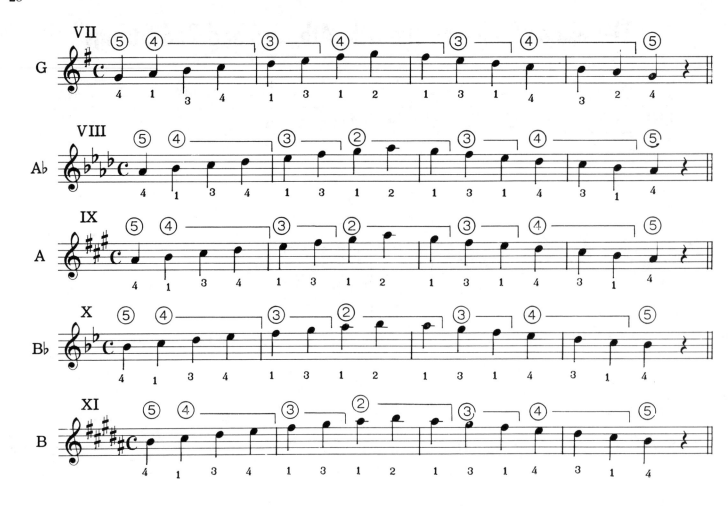

The Minor Scales on the 5th, 4th, 3rd and 2nd Strings

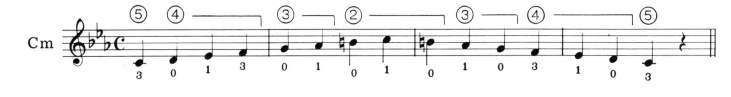

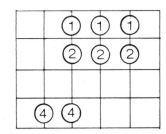

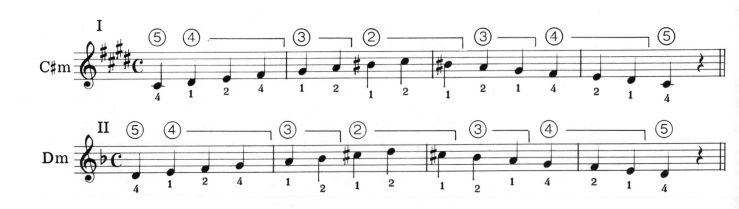

The Major to Tonic Minor Scales on the 5th, 4th, 3rd and 2nd Strings

The Major to Relative Minor Scales on the 5th, 4th, 3rd and 2nd Strings

The Major Scales on the 4th, 3rd, 2nd and 1st Strings

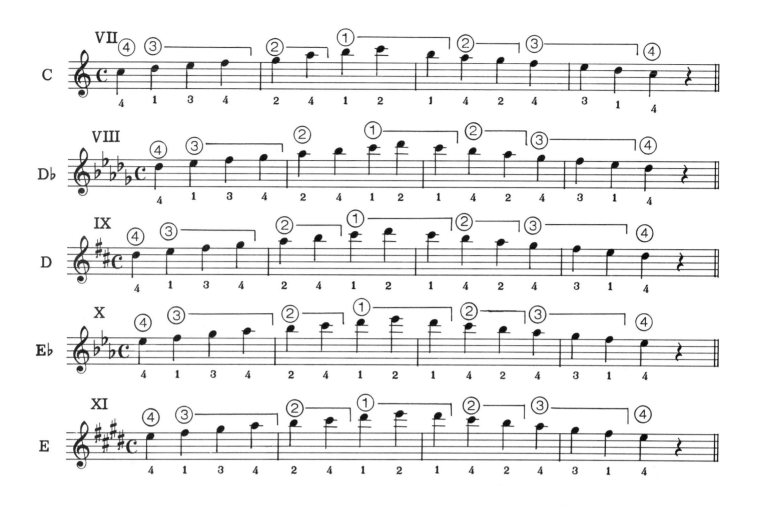

The Minor Scales on the 4th, 3rd, 2nd and 1st Strings

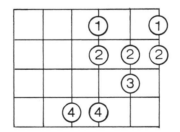

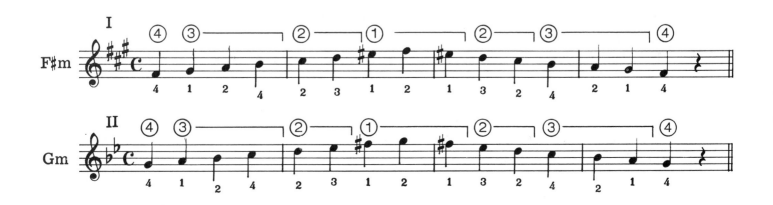

36

The Major to Tonic Minor Scales on the 4th, 3rd, 2nd and 1st Strings

38

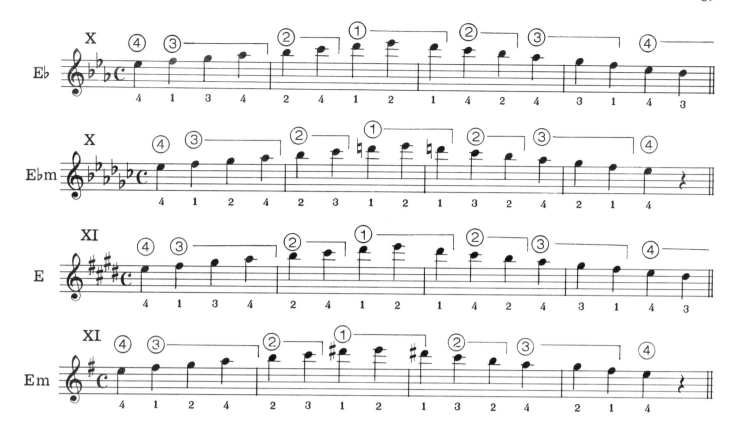

The Minor Scales on the 4th, 3rd, and 2nd Strings

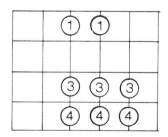

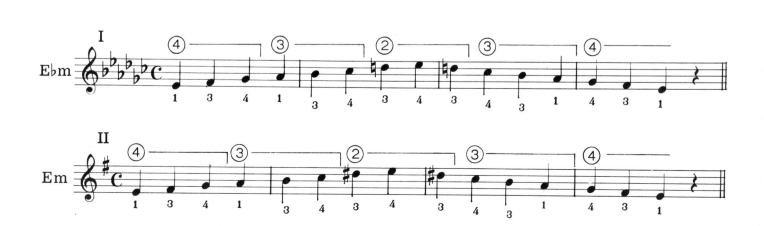

INTERVALS

An INTERVAL is the distance between two tones or the difference in pitch between two tones when sounded. Intervals are named according to the distance from the lower tone to the higher.

Intervals have NUMBER names and TYPE names. For example a 3rd could be major or minor depending upon the distance.

The staff degree occupied by the lower note and the staff degree occupied by the higher note are both included when determining the number name of the interval.

Below are nine intervals from C to each note in the C Scale.

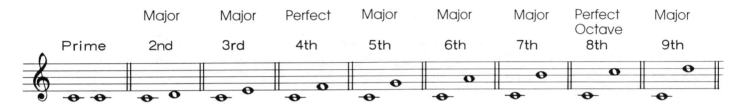

The Major to Relative Minor Scales

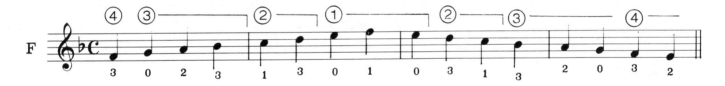

The Major Scales on All Six Strings
(Two Octaves)

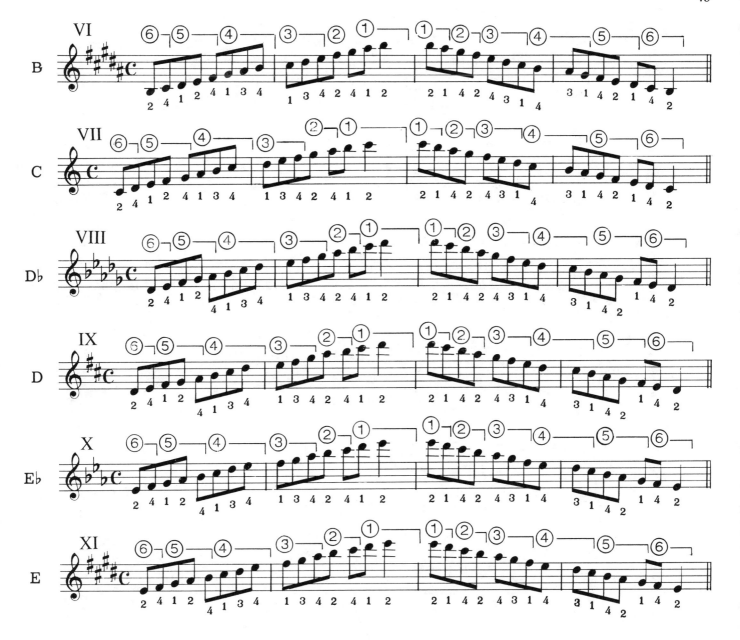

The Minor Scales

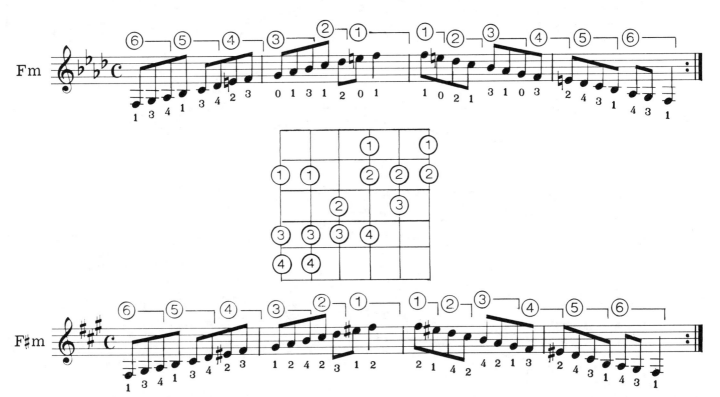

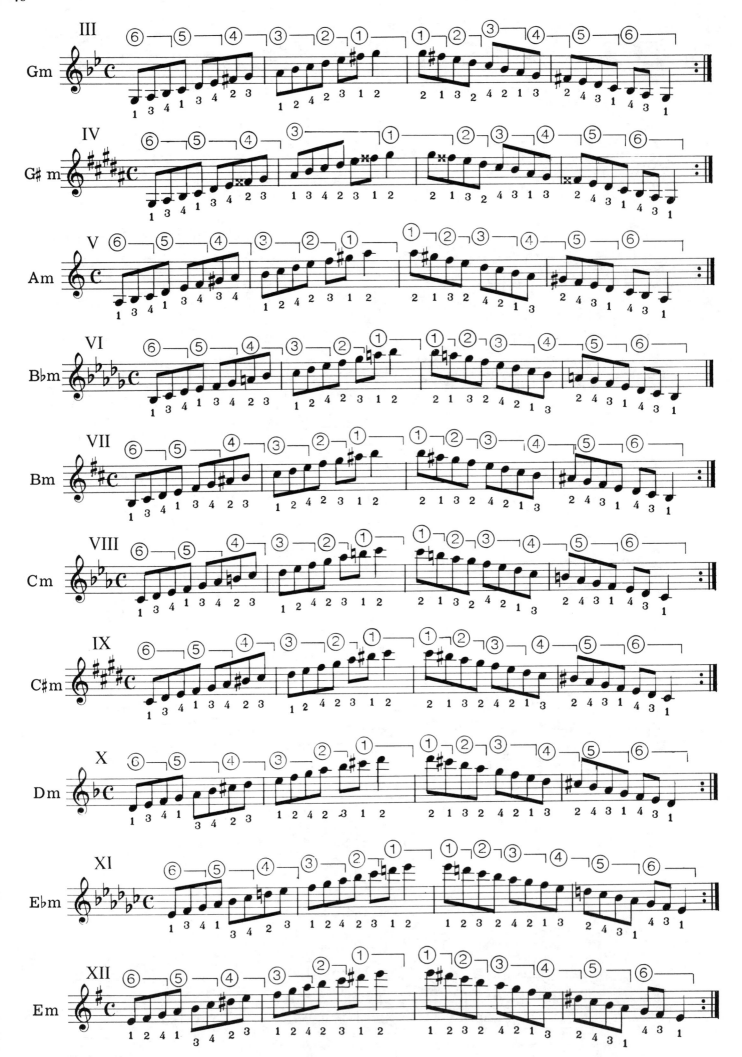

The Major to Tonic Minor Scales

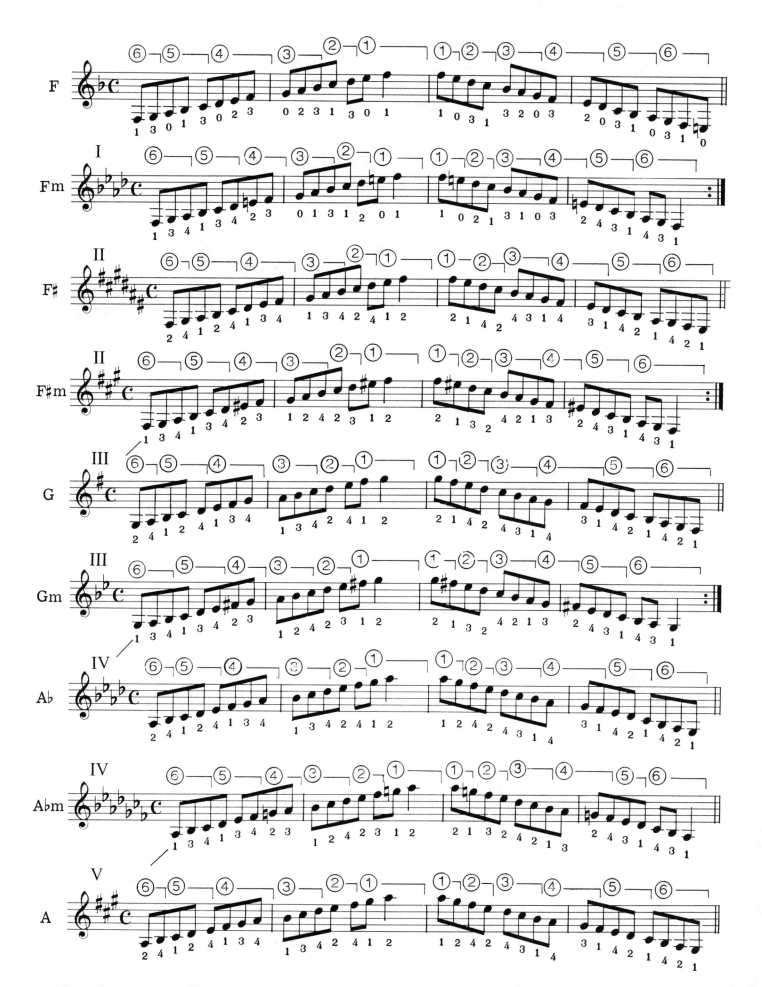

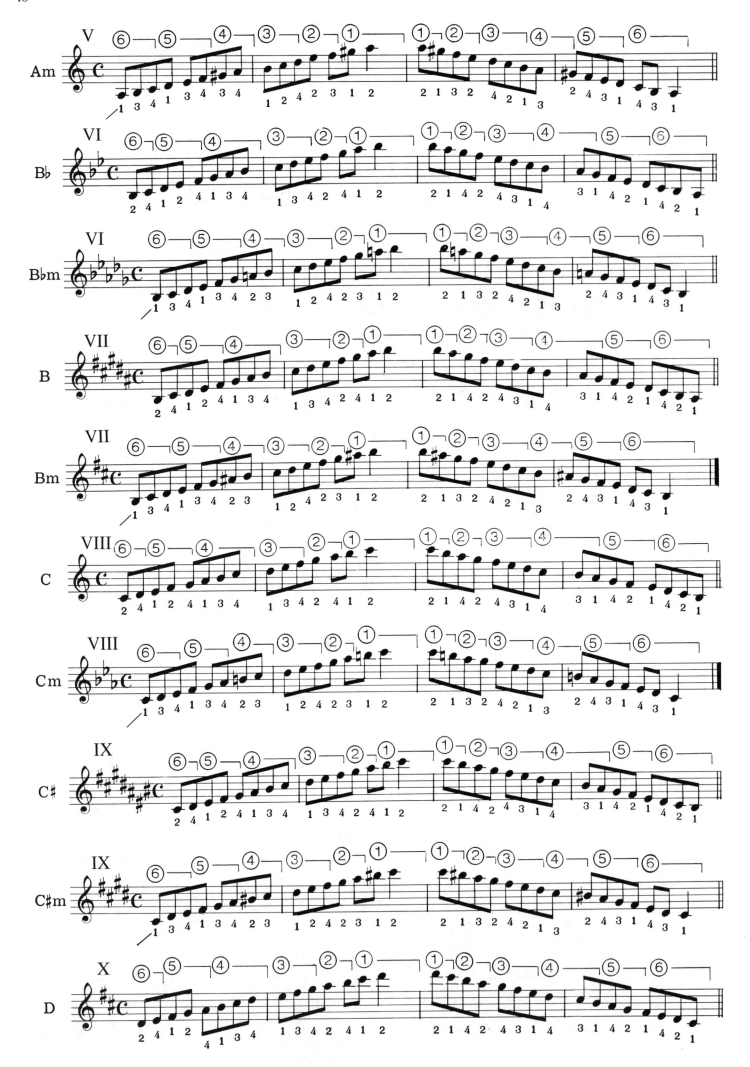

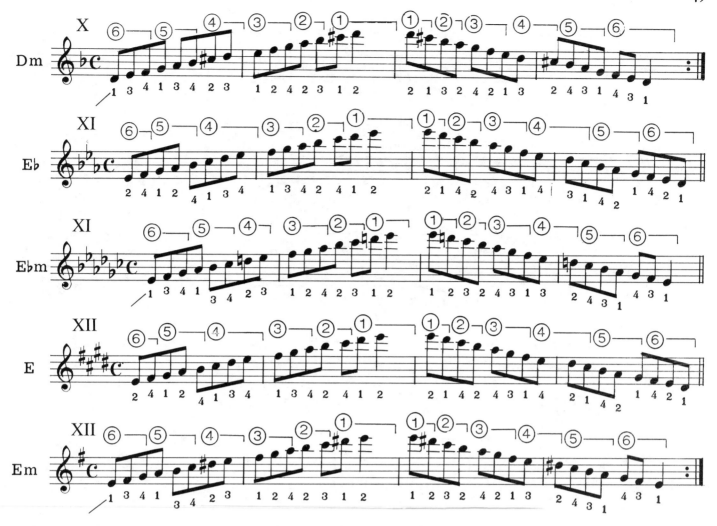

The Major to Relative Minor Scales

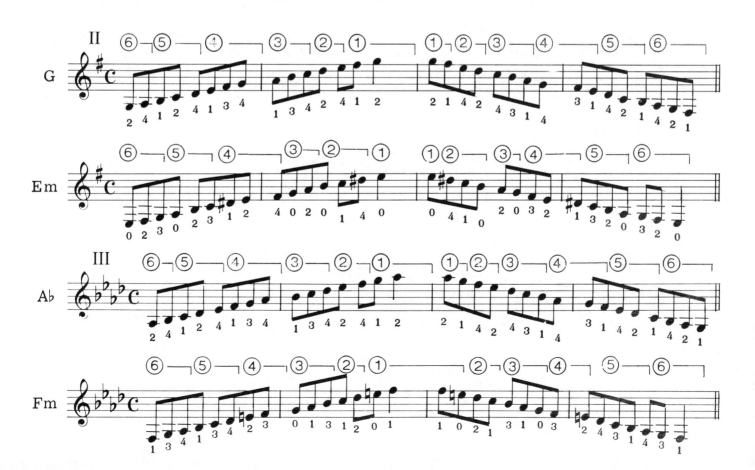

50

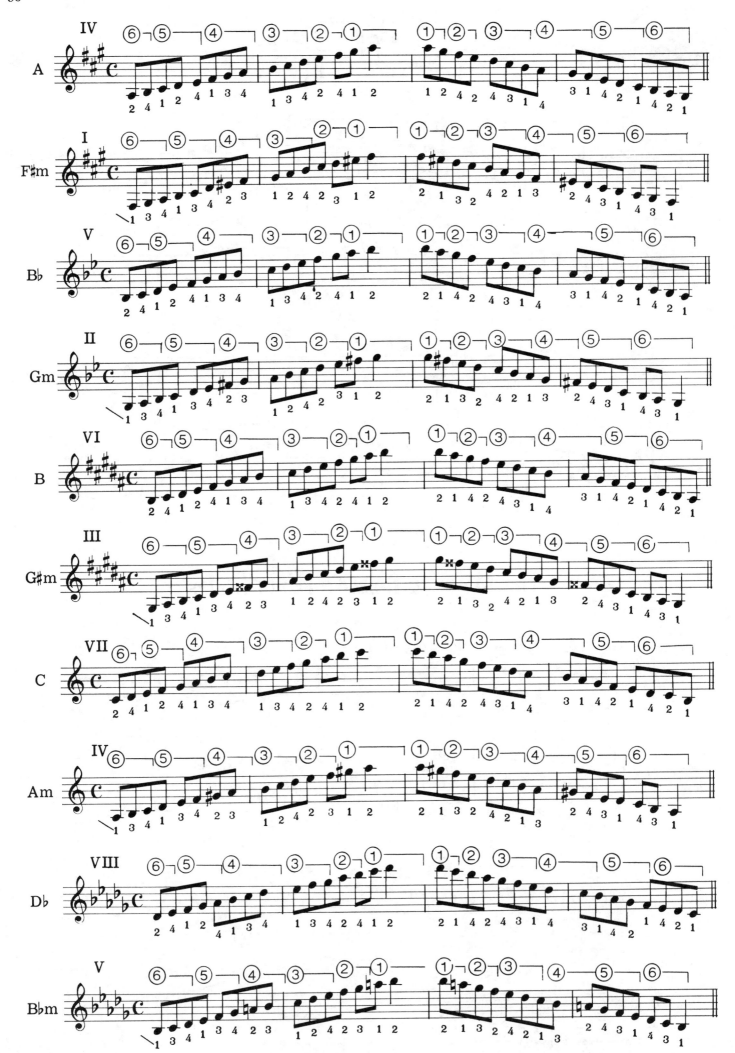

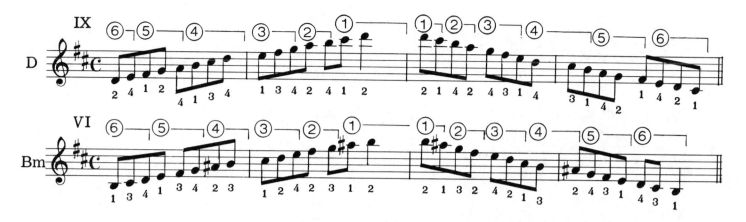

Continue upward for the Keys of E♭, Cm, E, C♯m, F and Dm.

The Two-Octave Scales on the 5th, 4th, 3rd, 2nd and 1st Strings

The Minor Scales on the 5th, 4th, 3rd, 2nd and 1st Strings
(Two Octaves)

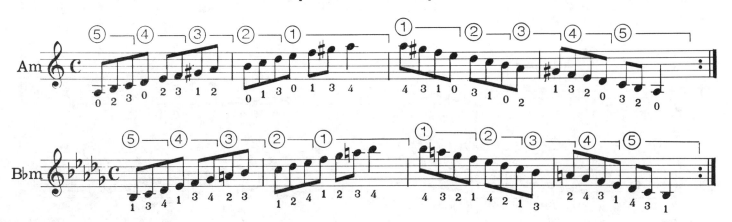

53

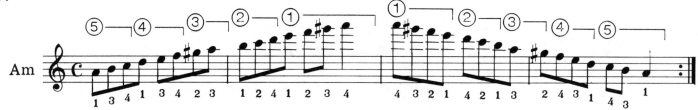

The Major to Tonic Minor Scales

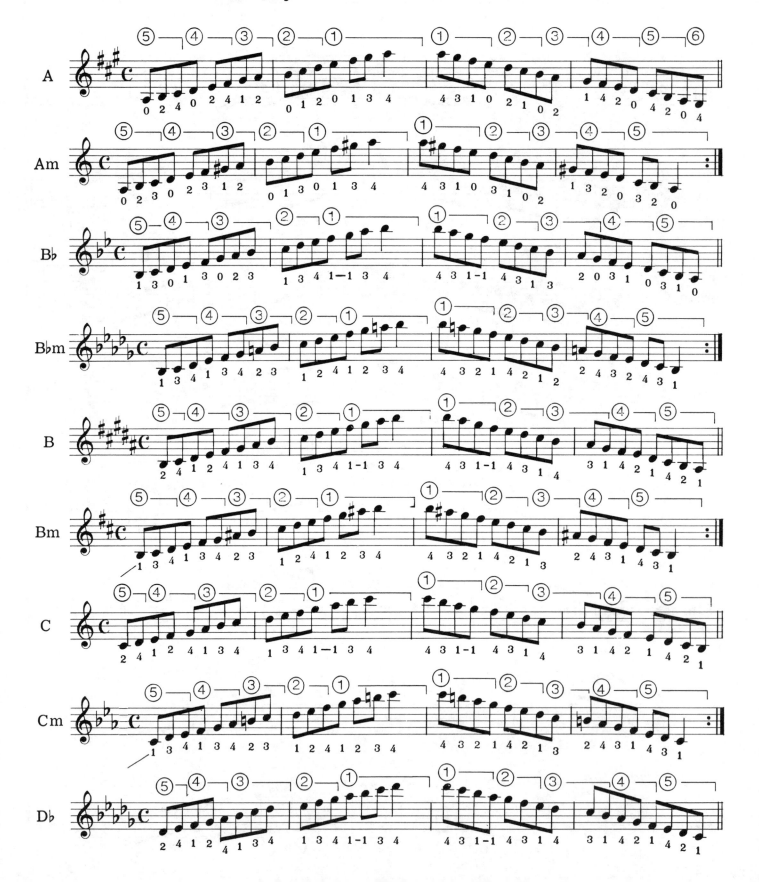

(ENHARMONIC) TO D♭m

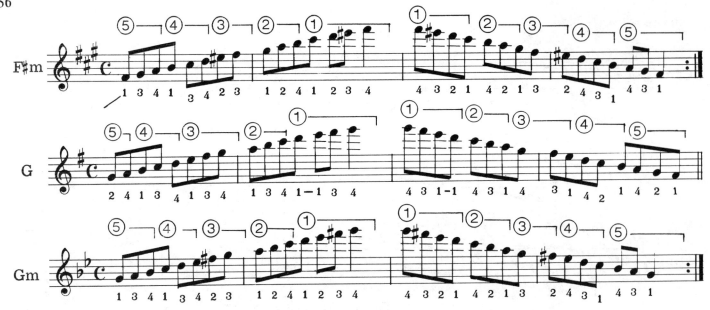

Another Two Octave Scale on All Six Strings

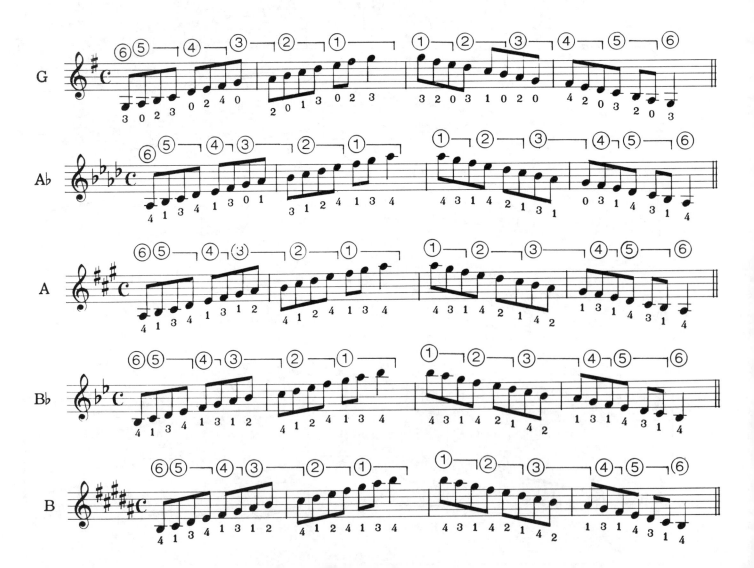

The Minor Scales

Major to Tonic Minor

60

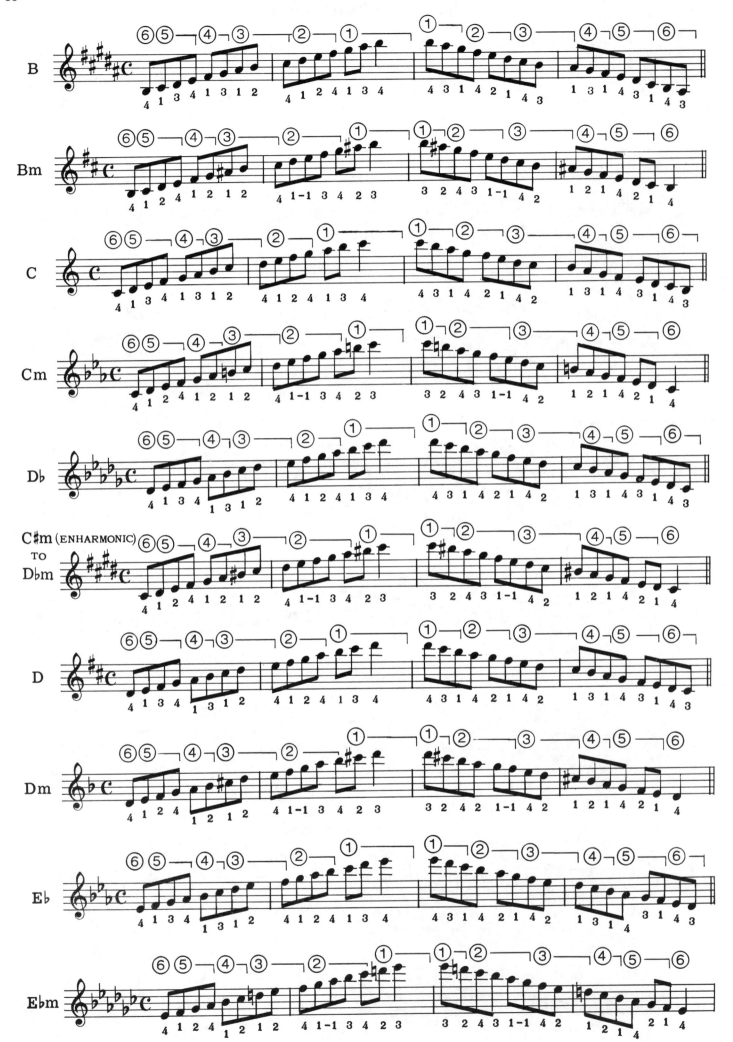

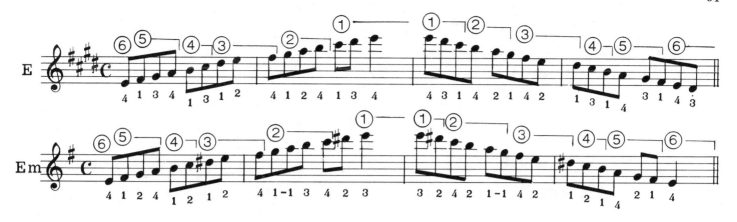

Another Major Scale in Two Octaves

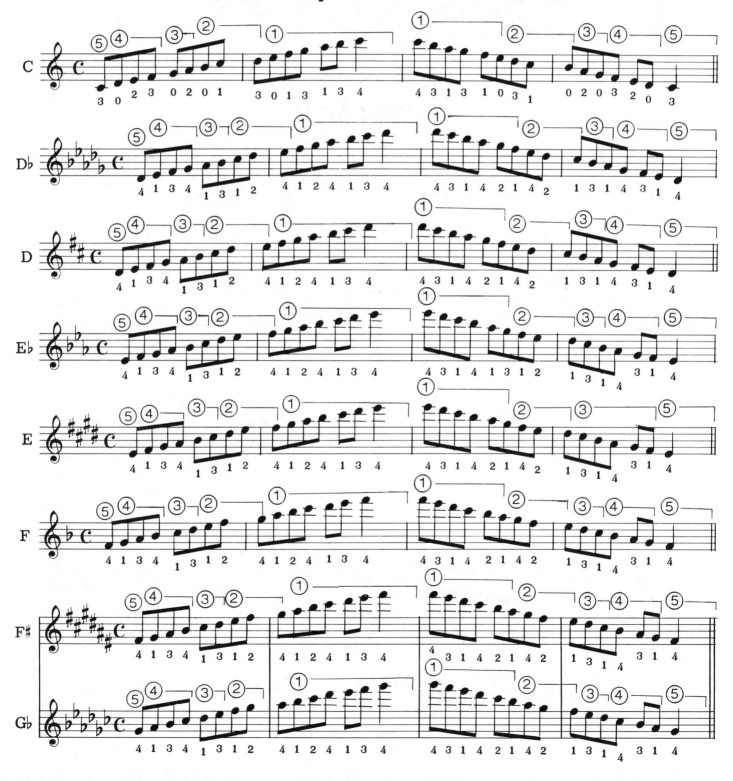

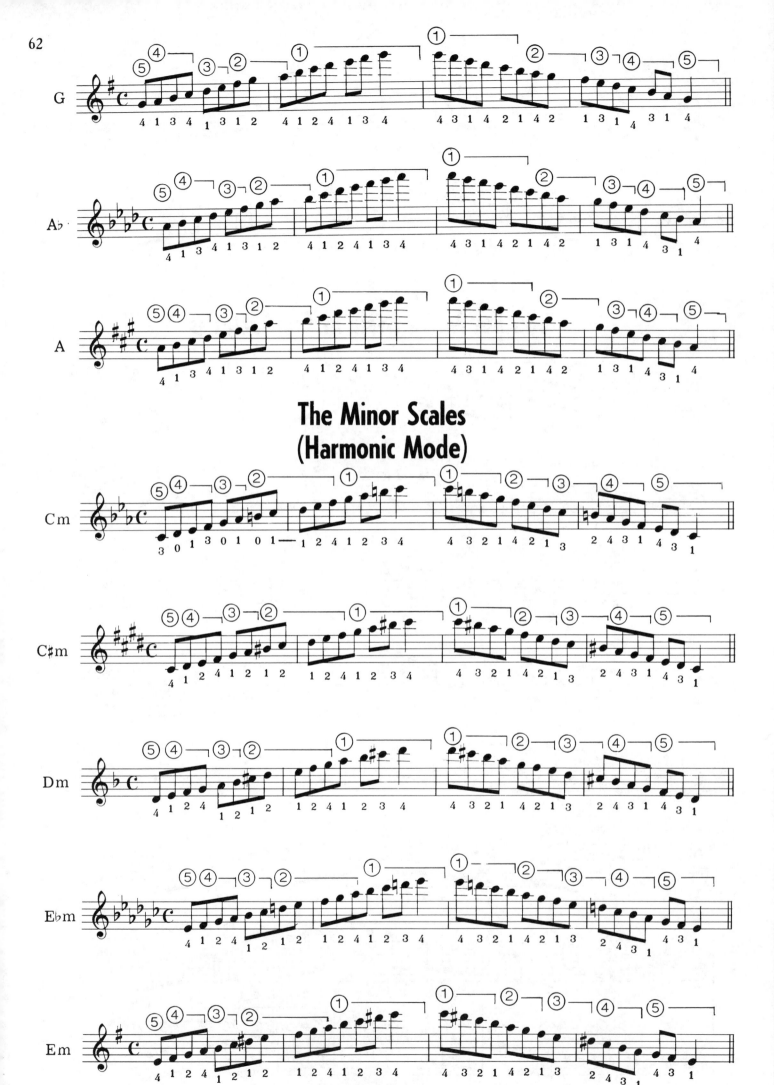

The Minor Scales
(Harmonic Mode)

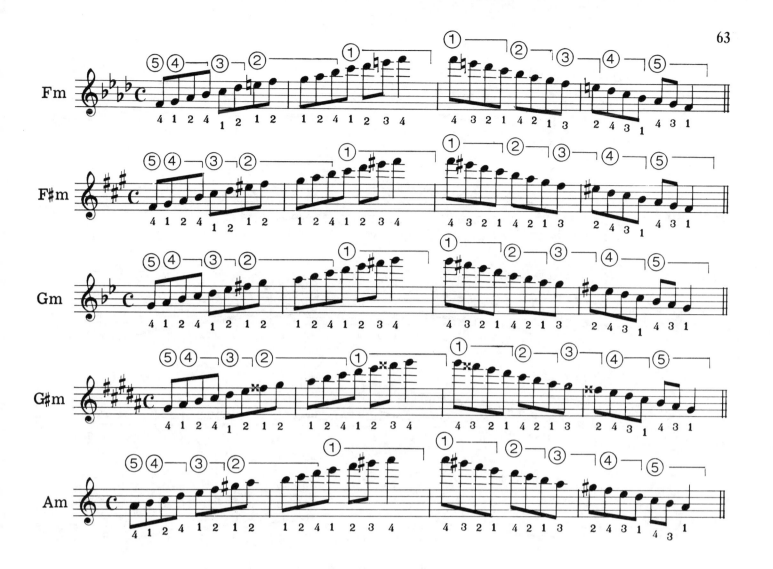

The Major to Tonic Minor Scales
(Two Octaves)

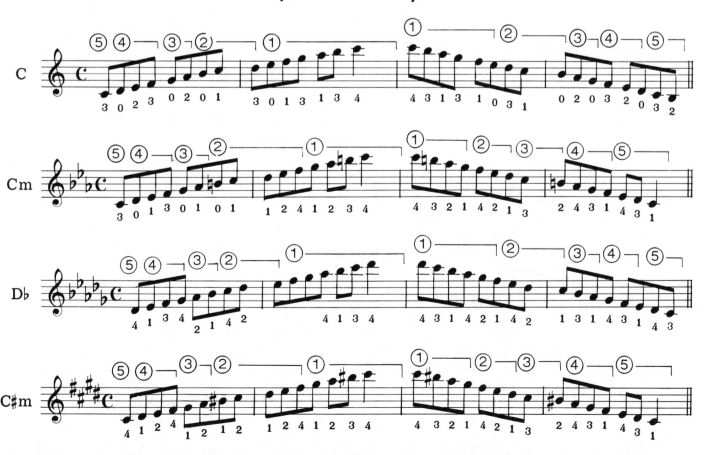

64

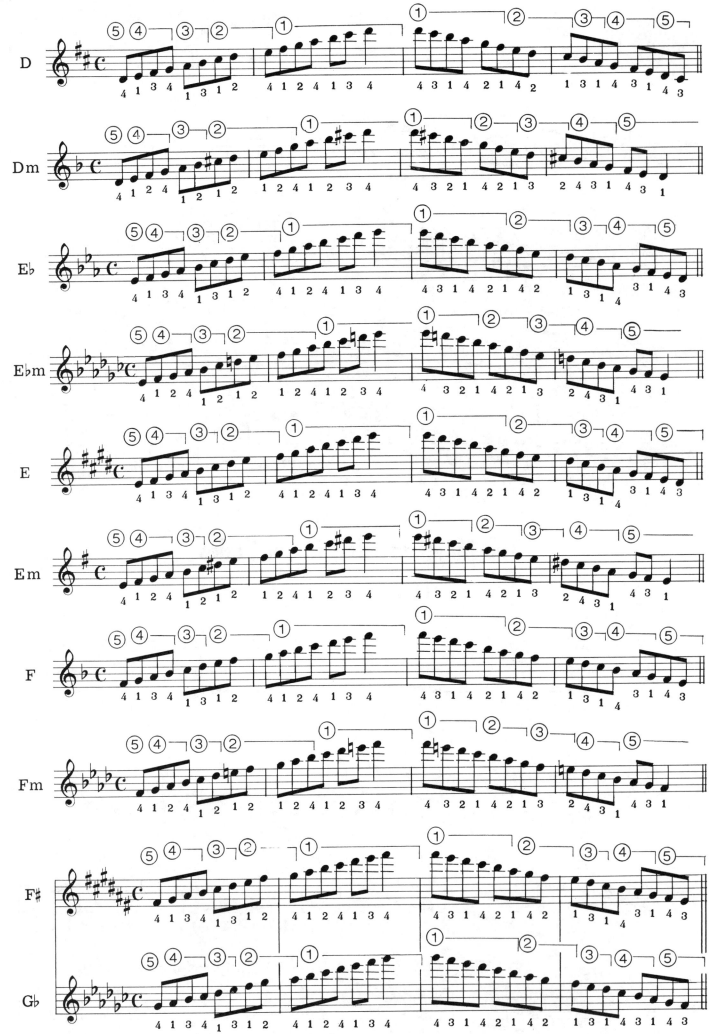

Major to Relative Minor

66

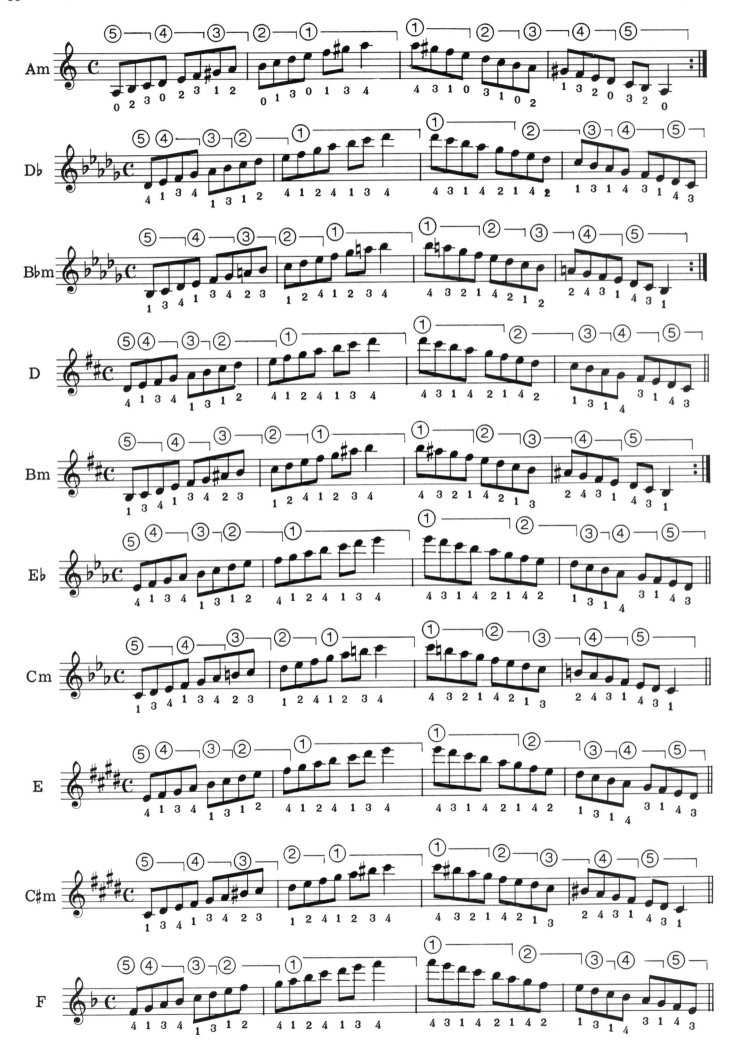

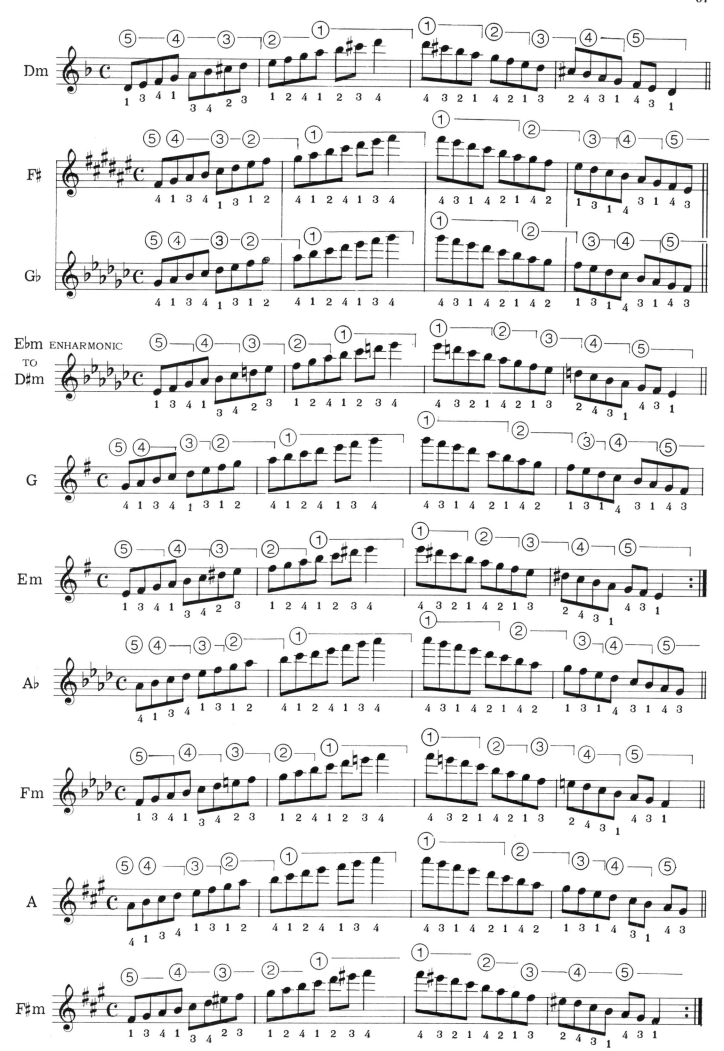

The Chromatic Scale

The Chromatic Scale is composed of *twelve half-steps* within an octave.
It may be written from any pitch; the Key-Signature will be that of the Major Key of the chosen pitch. It is written upward in sharps and downward in flats.

The Chromatic Scales on the 6th, 5th and 4th Strings

Play the above pattern up the fingerboard as far as feasible.

The Chromatic Scales on the 5th, 4th and 3rd Strings

Play the above scale pattern up the fingerboard.

The Chromatic Scales on the 4th, 3rd and 2nd Strings

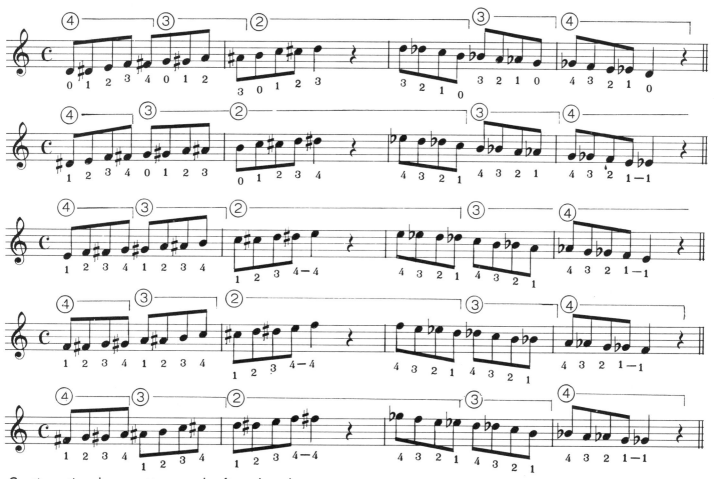

Continue the above pattern up the fingerboard

The Chromatic Scales on the 3rd, 2nd and 1st Strings

Continue the above form upward.

The Chromatic Scales on All Six Strings

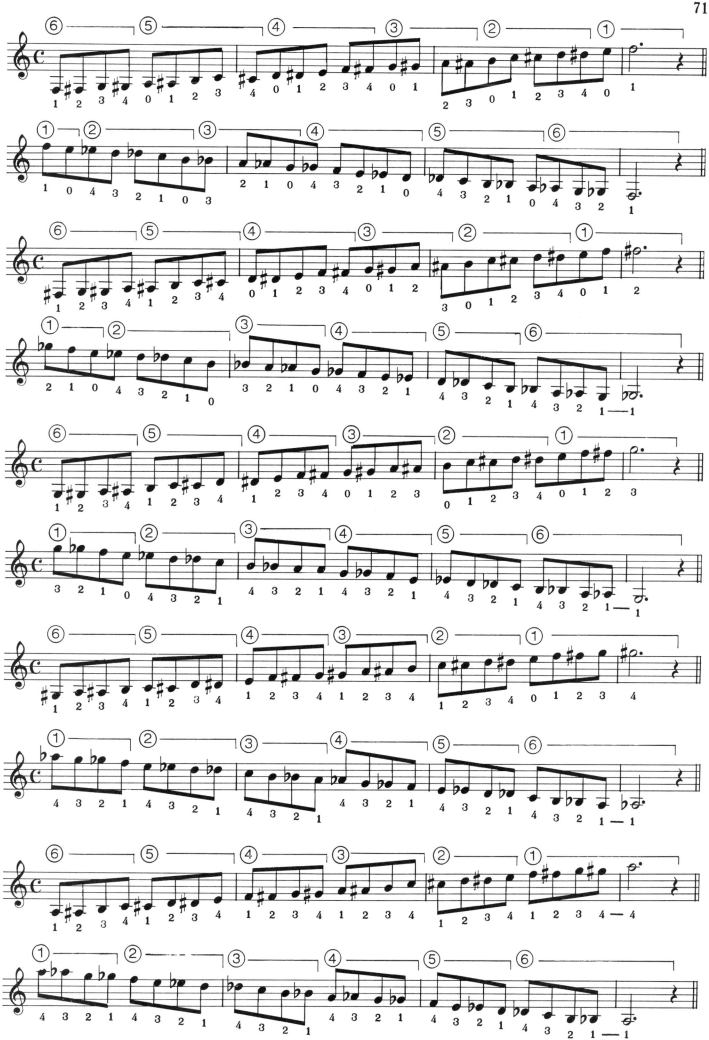

Continue the above scale form up the fingerboard.

The Whole-Tone Scales

The Whole-tone scale has the distance between each tone of one full step. There are six notes to the whole-tone scale. (Seven including the octave) The whole-tone scale can start on any tone.

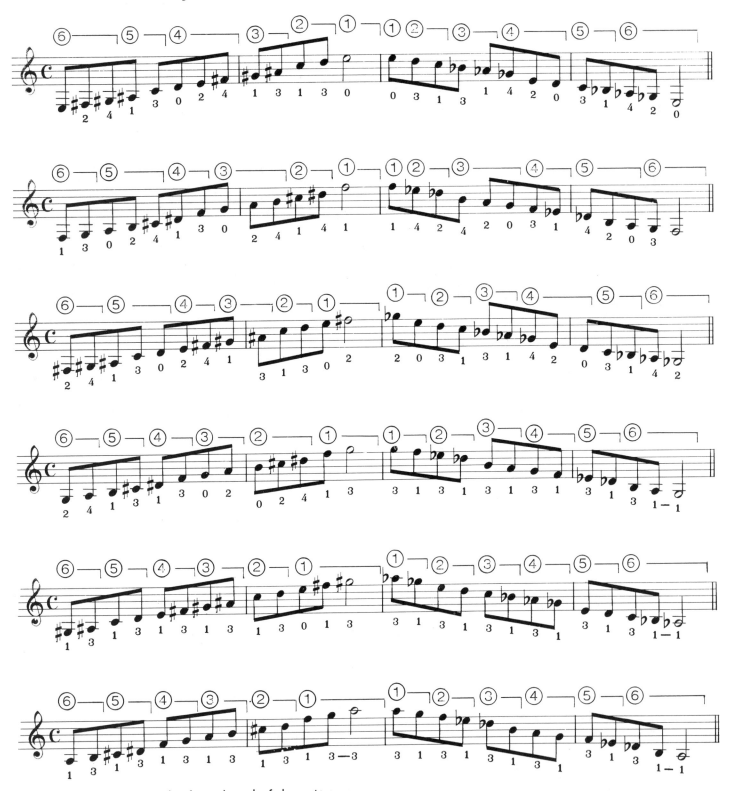

Practice the above up the fingerboard of the guitar.

For a complete study of the scales and arpeggios see *The Complete Book of Guitar Chords, Scales and Arpeggios* (MB94792).